## The Library of Writing Skills™

# A Step-by-Step Guide to
# Narrative Writing

Lauren Spencer

The Rosen Publishing Group, Inc., New York

*For every teacher who introduced me to*
*the wonder of words and storytelling*

Published in 2005 by The Rosen Publishing Group, Inc.
29 East 21st Street, New York, NY 10010

First Edition

**Library of Congress Cataloging-in-Publication Data**
Spencer, Lauren.
A step by step guide to narrative writing / Lauren Spencer.— 1st ed.
    p. cm. —  (The library of writing skills)
Includes bibliographical references and index.
ISBN 1-4042-0215-3 (library binding)
ISBN 1-4042-5307-6 (pbk.)
6-pack ISBN 1-4042-5313-0
1. English language—Rhetoric. 2. Narration (Rhetoric) 3. Report writing.
I. Title. II. Series: Spencer, Lauren, Library of writing skills.
PE1425.S64 2005
808'.042—dc22
                                                            2004002687

*Manufactured in the United States of America*

# Table of Contents

# Introduction

Everyone's got a tale to tell. And whether it's an incident that's actually happened or one that's a complete fantasy, the stories that exist in our minds are begging to be set free. Releasing them from our imaginations and memories can be achieved through narrative writing, a form of storytelling that brings the audience into the author's world. The best narrative moments are often those in which readers find themselves nodding their heads and thinking, "I've been there," or "Wow, that sounds amazing," because the story paints such a realistic picture of the experience.

Often referred to as expository writing, narrative writing opens the door of a situation and exposes the events inside. As with any creative writing, one's ability to show an event unfold through the use of interesting details is crucial. This narrative art is achieved with the use of pacing, characterization, dialogue, and action. A narrative piece needs a strong foundation on which to construct its story.

In this book, we will examine all the elements needed to get the creative process moving, including choosing an idea, firming up the plot, and strengthening the narrative voice. Another topic discussed will be the process of working with others on a final draft in order to achieve the best possible story. We will also explore various literary techniques and how they can enhance your writing when combined with basic story elements.

Narrative writing often allows the author to tell a tale by revisiting a scene out of his or her own life. Narratives can also take on a fictional viewpoint. Whatever the choice, a narrative tale is one that offers insight into the mind of an author and the heart of his or her story.

# Prewriting

In narrative writing, an author has a chance to make his or her mark on the world by relating a story that only he or she can tell. Whether it comes from a personal experience or is one that the writer has imagined, the point of a narrative is to bring one's subject to life. By using sensory details, the five *W*s and *H* (who, what, where, when, why, and how), and basic story structure, any subject can be made exciting.

A personal narrative is based on an event in the author's life. It is written in the first person, using the pronoun "I," since the event is being told from the author's point of view. Ideas for personal narratives can come from thinking about places you've been, people you know or have known, and experiences that have affected your life.

Fictional narratives are stories that are made up and are written in the third person (he, she, or it). This

## KEY

✔ **Read various personal accounts and fictional stories and then think about the differences between these two types of narrative.**

✔ **Think about various narrative topics to write about.**

✔ **Gather ideas and information to support your choice of subjects.**

is when an author chooses to step outside of an event and describe it from a distance by using another point of view. The third person is also commonly used when an author creates a fictional story. Sometimes an author will take a personal experience and fictionalize it by creating a character and enhancing his or her actions with details that never happened. Or the topic might be one that the author has created based on something he or she read, observed, or overheard.

Whether personal or fictional, a narrative requires a clearly written beginning, middle, and end. As the writer, you are the narrator of the story. It is your responsibility to take the reader on a detailed journey so that he or she can truly experience what you're describing.

# Gathering Ideas

When it comes to topics for narratives, personal experiences are rife with possibilities. Think about times when you just couldn't wait to share with someone an event that happened. Call up memories that gave you new insights or different perspectives on a person, place, or thing.

Next, think of details that will make the incident believable for whomever is reading the story. If you need your memory jogged, search through old notebooks, journals, or photo albums.

Think about past vacations you might have had, or the first time you experienced something that was especially important to you. Very often, conversations with others will also remind you of details that could turn out to be fantastic additions to your story.

For fictional ideas, you can use the same methods you would use to write a piece about a personal experience, or you can look to alternative sources. Writers often keep a file of clippings from newspapers, magazines, and other sources to draw inspiration for future writing projects.

Another great way to capture ideas is to carry a small notebook, index cards, or scrap paper around with you to jot down ideas for both personal and fictional narratives. These moments can range from odd or interesting things that you see around you, to something you've over-heard. They are fragments of thoughts, rarely complete sentences. Things like "Man on the bus singing along to his stereo loudly while people stare" or "A purple poodle being walked by a blue-haired senior citizen." Direct observations about life make writing colorful and truthful.

Recording interesting incidents will help you to create engaging details for current stories, or help to inspire future ones. Intriguing details can appear out of nowhere and catch your eye. Recording these moments is an invaluable writing tool.

## ASK YOURSELF

☐ Do I have a clear focus for my narrative, whether it's based on personal experience or imagined?

☐ Have I mapped out interesting details to include in my story?

☐ Do I feel connected to my topic?

☐ Am I ready to start writing?

To narrow your topic choices, make a list of your options on a sheet of paper. Examine them and pick one that holds the most promise for engaging sights, sounds, and details to sustain the story from beginning to end. The idea needs to be focused so that you're not attempting to

## People Watching

Grab a small notebook or note cards and head out to your local park. Notice everything (and everyone) around you. Find a comfortable place to sit and concentrate on your thoughts. Next, observe your surroundings for about five to ten minutes, just watching and listening to your environment. What do you see, hear, and smell? Can you hear birds singing? Can you see children playing? Or maybe the park is deserted except for a group of older folks feeding pigeons. Whatever the sights and sounds are, jot them down in your notebook.

Next, try to notice details that are more specific. Perhaps the park is deserted because it is in a state of disrepair. If so, note its condition. Is it a dismal, cold day or are there hot, sweaty kids running around a public fountain or pool? Any incidents and details you can notice are fair game. Practice freewriting these observations for about fifteen minutes without stopping.

cram too many ideas into one piece. For example, a subject like "my first year at middle school" is too broad. Unless you are writing a lengthy paper, a topic like that one may prove to be overwhelming. However, you can always take a broad topic and whittle it down.

Instead of attempting to write about your experiences over an entire school year, perhaps focus only on your first day, week, or month. Concentrating on a more specific period will help you hone in on the mood of your piece. By doing this, you will write about events with specificity and detail, grabbing your reader's attention with an identifying experience.

Trimming your focus will also help you manage the content of your entire narrative. Once you've chosen your topic, you'll want to have what you need to build your story. If you're writing a personal narrative, then gather any notes that you have made or pictures you have collected about your experience. For a fictional piece, assemble notes about things that you've looked up or read about the topic. Since narrative writing sprouts from your own mind and doesn't depend heavily on research, your notes will likely be limited.

A good way to organize your ideas is with a chart that maps who, what, where, when, why, and how regarding the main character and the situation unfolding. These five *Ws* and *H* are the thread that weaves together the narrative structure and establishes the foundation for your story.

## Five *Ws* and *H* Chart

Write your subject at the top of a blank sheet of paper and then mark off six columns across the page. Devote one column to each of your five *Ws* and *H*; then begin your notes. You are using the five *Ws* and *H* to focus on and organize the following points regarding the story's main character: Who the story is about; what is happening to the main character; when it happened; where the character is; and why the character is there. You can also add how the character arrived at this situation.

EXAMPLE:
### My First Day at Middle School

| Who | What | When | Where | Why | How |
|-----|------|------|-------|-----|-----|
| Me | It was my first day at middle school | Two years ago | Ulster Middle School | I was starting sixth grade | On my bicycle |
|  | I got lost going to my math class and was late | On a windy September day | A ten-minute bike ride from my house | I was in a new town |  |

## Sensory Chart

|  | Me | Teacher | Students | School |
|---|---|---|---|---|
| **Looks** | Favorite sneakers; jeans; blue T-shirt | Skirt; hair pulled back; funny shoes | Mostly wearing jeans & T-shirts some girls in dresses & skirts | Three stories; made of red brick with a flagpole |
| **Sounds** | Quiet | Firm | Loud yelling and laughter | Loud with people in the hallways |
| **Feels** | Nervous | Happy because she was smiling; in control because she sounded strict | Don't know how they felt; some looked nervous, some comfortable | Hallways were cold |
| **Smells** | A little sweat | Like perfume | Don't know | The halls smelled like food |

# Sensory Details

You can use sensory elements to describe how all the characters look, sound, feel (emotionally and physically), and even smell. This will pave the way for your first draft by mapping out the cast of characters and the action involved.

Draw another chart and fill in the characters and main setting of your story along the top. Write your sensory list down the left-hand side. Then fill in details wherever you are able. Complete this chart using first impressions and memories. Record as many details as you can, and remember, since this is your narrative story, there's no such thing as a wrong answer.

# Writing the First Draft

When writing a narrative piece, the point of view you use to engage the reader is very important. Point of view is the position, or slant, from which a story is told.

If this is a personal narrative, then it will be written from your perspective, using the first person "I" to explain the action. Example:

> I was nervous on the first day of school. I walked into Mrs. Barker's class and headed for the back of the room. I could feel her staring at me from her desk. There was a dark-haired boy moving around near the windows and I hoped he wouldn't talk to me.

## KEY

✔ **Focus on the narrator's point of view.**

✔ **Plan the structure of the piece.**

✔ **Write the first draft.**

For fictional narratives, there are some point-of-view choices.

**Omniscient** (all-knowing): The narrator describes the thoughts of all the characters in the story. Example:

> Mrs. Barker smiled to herself as she watched Sheila walk into the classroom. She knew how scary it must be for her as a new student. Sheila did feel nervous and headed for the back of the room, hoping that no one would notice her. Meanwhile, John sat in his familiar desk near the window so he could stare outside, just like he did last year.

**Limited Omniscient:** The narrator can only tell the thoughts and feelings of the main character. Example:

> Sheila felt nervous on her first day at the new school. As she took her seat in Mrs. Barker's classroom, she wondered what surprises the teacher might have in store. She also noticed a dark-haired boy near the window and she hoped that he wouldn't notice her.

**Camera View** (objective): The narrator tells the story, but he or she doesn't share any thoughts or feelings about the characters. Example:

> Sheila walked into Mrs. Barker's classroom and sat down at a desk in the back. A dark-haired boy near the window was moving desks. She looked at Mrs. Barker, who was standing stiffly at the front of the classroom.

Once a point of view is selected, then it's time to look at how the events in the piece will fit together. In narrative writing, the basic elements of a story establish its foundation. While the location, characters, and central point of the piece have already been decided during the prewriting process, now is the time to fill out the action. Before you begin writing your first draft, try charting a plot guide to determine your path. A "story map" will launch you directly into your writing project. Don't worry about filling in every space or going in any particular order, just let the ideas in your head loose onto the chart. Specific details will be filled in as your writing progresses. The purpose of this chart is to create an outline of your story's main points. Unless you are particularly smitten with your title, you will now choose what is known as a "working title." This temporary title is often revised before the final draft.

# The Order of Things

Once you've established the setting, characters, and events in your narrative, you can examine various ways to present them so that your story flows from one moment to the next. This is called a plot line. It follows the action of your

## Story Map

**Working Title:** My First Day in a New School

**Setting:**      A classroom

**Characters:**   Me
Other students
Mrs. Barker

**Problem:**

**Event 1:** I thought I was late for my first class because I didn't know where the classroom was and wandered in the hallways.

**Event 2:** I felt embarrassed because everyone was staring at me so I walked really fast and tripped.

**Event 3:** When I finally found my classroom, it turned out I wasn't late. There was only one other student in the room (John) and he wasn't paying attention to me—he was moving desks around.

**Event 4:** I found a desk near the back of the room and saw the teacher looking at me.

**Event 5:** More students entered the classroom and stared at me.

**Event 6:** I dropped my book on the floor.

**Solution:** _____
_____
_____

story. Sometimes a writer will start the plot line directly in the middle of the action in order to draw the reader in and add any background information once the action is established. The plot line of any narrative has five parts: exposition (usually background information like the setting and characters); rising action (central part of the story that introduces the conflict); climax (the story's turning point); falling action (actions that lead to the story's ending); and resolution (the story's conclusion). Example:

> Suddenly there was a loud "boom," and all eyes were on me. I turned bright red and looked at my 400-page history book lying on the floor. I had accidentally pushed it off my desk as I tried to open my notebook. Mrs. Barker stopped talking and the room was totally silent. Since this was my first day in this school, I didn't know what to expect. Would the teacher yell? Would the students laugh? I was so embarrassed that I felt like crying.

Other options for the order of your piece are chronological—explaining the event forward or backward in time—or physically from top to bottom or from bottom to top. Example:

## Potential Plot Lines:

### Chronologically Forward:

> I woke up that morning knowing that today I'd have to face a new school, new teachers, and new

students. I got out of bed slowly and began getting dressed. After eating breakfast, I walked to the front door with heavy feet.

*Chronologically Backward:*

It was finally over. My first day at a new school was filled with drama. When the final bell rang and I left the building, I could only breathe a sigh of relief. Looking back, I remembered all the things that had happened during the last eight torturous hours.

*Physically from Top to Bottom:*

Ulster Middle School was a huge building. As I looked up at all three stories, I realized just how nervous I was about my first day of school. The place looked very clean, and the students going through the door to their classes seemed at ease and joyful. I felt really out of place.

Once you have decided on a vision for your narrative piece, begin writing your first draft. In order to maintain the flow of your work, don't stop writing unless you need to check your notes or examine your charts for details. Keep your words spilling onto the page as your story takes shape. Don't

## Take a Ride

Imagine you are on a magic carpet that can take you anywhere you want to go. Using details and the five *Ws* and one *H*, write at least one paragraph describing the experience.

Now write it again, but this time from the point of view of the magic carpet with you on it. Be sure you use all five *Ws* and one *H*.

worry about its length since you'll have a chance to shape it later. Keep the flow going until you feel the action is winding down. Don't worry about spelling or grammar now, since you will make those corrections later.

Now that you are familiar with the elements of a plot line, consider developing the framework for a longer narrative, or expand the piece you are currently working on. Think specifically about the importance of expositional information such as the story's setting and how it affects your characters. In what time does your story take place? Perhaps it is set in the future or in the past. If so, how will this information

## ASK YOURSELF

☐ Have I included all the basic elements in my narrative story?

☐ Is there a clear point of view and order to my writing?

☐ Have I incorporated the information from my prewriting charts?

impact your characters? Will they have characteristics that seem unusual to the reader? Perhaps consider including these less obvious details to help readers more fully understand the circumstances of your story. Descriptive details can make the difference when trying to maintain the allusion of a specific time and place. Practice expanding the expositional information in your draft. This includes the details about each of your characters and their relationships to each other.

A standard plot line contains five parts:

## 1. Exposition:
When the setting, characters, and conflict are introduced.

## 2. Rising Action:
The focus of the story as the main character tries to solve the problem.

## 3. Climax:
Often the turning point of the story, it is the most important or exciting moment in the piece.

## 4. Falling Action:
The time in the story when the ending or resolution is near.

## 5. Resolution:
When the problem or conflict is worked out, or the event has passed, signaling the end of the story.

# Adding Style

Now that the first version of your narrative story is drafted, it's a good time to notice where additional details can be added to give the piece more style. Describe your setting and characters by using the five senses. Examine your writing and find areas where information that electrifies the senses—such as sight, sound, touch, smell, and taste—can be added. This will add details that are unique to your story.

Figures of speech, which are writing techniques that form "word pictures," are a great way to "show" an element in a story.

One example of a figure of speech is hyperbole, which is the use of extreme exaggeration. Hyperbole is used to stretch an element of truth in order to add extra emphasis to the message. In the following example, a fictional character narrates a moment in the lunchroom in which the exaggeration is built on the truth that she is hungry. Example:

## KEY

✔ **Support your story with descriptive and sensory-inspired details.**

✔ **Understand stylistic elements that will engage the reader.**

✔ **Fine-tune character descriptions.**

> Kristen stood impatiently in the lunch
> line waiting for her turn. Her stomach
> was rumbling so loudly with hunger that
> she was sure people in China could hear it.

Another figure of speech is called personification, in which something that is not human is brought to life. This technique adds an imaginative twist to narrative stories. Example:

> When she reached the front of the
> line, Kristen thought that the mini
> pizzas were smiling at her with
> pepperoni mouths.

# Dialogue

The expressions between characters in stories are called dialogue. Quotation marks are used to set this dialogue apart from the rest of the text. Quoted speech adds another dimension to narrative writing by allowing the characters to speak for themselves. Unless it is necessary that you quote a long speech word for word, it's best to keep dialogue limited to a few sentences. Using dialogue in this way allows the story to have momentum. Dialogue should be just long enough to add a layer of detail. If a quoted passage lasts for too long, it usually sounds unrealistic. Although people often say, "Write like

## ASK YOURSELF

☐ Am I ready to revise my piece by adding figurative language?

☐ Do I fully understand the use of quotation marks so that I can add dialogue to my narrative?

☐ Am I willing to go to the core of the character's feelings in order to add depth to my story?

you speak," this message has to do with an author's ability to bring his or her individual personality to the writing. If you listen to yourself or others during conversations, you will notice pauses and slang words. You only want to include these elements in your written work in moderation. In most cases, they are used only to fill out a character description. If slang words are overused, your characters will sound sloppy. This is not to imply that you need to change the meaning or tone of what someone says in order to include that quote, but clean up the embarrassing bits. To understand how quoted material is altered from everyday speech to the written word, try tape recording a dinner conversation without anyone knowing it. Afterward, listen to the recording. Then determine how you can write down exactly what has been said by using complete thoughts and punctuation without changing the meaning of the moment. Example:

**Original conversation:**

"Did ya, um, hear about how Kristen's lunch table was broken?" asked my brother.

**Corrected text:**

"Did you hear about Kristen's broken lunch table?" asked my brother.

Reading examples of spoken passages from favorite books is a great way to understand the power of dialogue. When used correctly, it never fails to enhance a scene or add emphasis. Always remember to set off spoken dialogue with quotation marks, which surround the exact words of the speaker. Quotation marks are also used before and after words seen on signs or billboards. Example:

> Kristen said to the lunch lady, "I'll take three mini pizzas please." Afterward she replied, "Thank you." Then she walked over to her regular table and saw a sign that read "Broken." She looked around and realized that there was no place left to sit.

If you want to capture the essence of what someone has said without using his or her exact words, you can paraphrase. This means you can eliminate the need for quotation marks by reworking a spoken passage in your own words. Example:

> Kristen asked the lunch lady for three mini pizzas. After she had thanked her, Kristen turned around and realized that her favorite lunch table was broken. She had no place to sit.

# What's Inside

A deeper sense of your characters will develop when you open a window into their minds. Character development also brings texture to whatever incident is unfolding. There are a few different ways to write about the goings-on inside of a character. This is called inner dialogue because it's as if the character were talking to him or herself. Such reflection about a situation can bring the reader closer to a character's feelings. Example:

> As Kristen walked away from the broken table, she wished that she were invisible. She didn't want anyone to see how embarrassed she was carrying around her little pizzas with nowhere to eat them. She hated the fact that she was the first one of her group to arrive. Now she had to stand around waiting for the others.

Another way to express inner feelings about your characters is through flashbacks, which call up memories as a reminder of something that's happened earlier. Example:

> Having nowhere to eat her lunch reminded Kristen of her first day at this school two years ago. Back then, she didn't know anyone and had dreaded lunch period because she always had to sit alone.

Flash forwarding anticipates possibilities about how a situation could unfold based on the thoughts of the character. Example:

> Kristen's mind raced ahead. What if her friends never showed up for lunch and she was forced to stand here holding her mini pizzas while they got cold?

Foreshadowing serves as a warning about something that will happen later in the story. It is like dropping a clue about a future event. Example:

> When she saw her team captain coming toward her, Kristen should have known that lunch period was not going to go the way she wanted it to.

Inner dialogue can also take the form of a conversation back and forth inside one character's head as he or she explores all the possibilities of the moment. Quotation marks are used for the main thought as if it's being said out loud. Example:

> "Maybe I'll just go outside and sit down," Kristen thought. She suddenly panicked, wondering what would happen if she left and then all of her friends showed up. They might think that she had ditched them. Or what if a table became empty right after she stepped out? She knew that she was probably over-reacting, but she was hungry and annoyed.

Try approaching your narrative draft by including some inner dialogue. You'll be surprised about how much information you can relate to the reader by using this method.

# Revising Your First Draft

The act of revision is so much more than merely copying your work neatly and correcting your spelling and grammar mistakes. Although those tasks are a part of the final preparation before your story can be shared, there is another essential step to take first. This involves revising and polishing the details of your story. The word "revise" comes from the French word *revisere*, which means " to look at again."

This process of observation is where you, the author, examine your writing with a critical eye. This is the time to figure out what can be added or changed to make the piece more interesting. You are like an explorer who, having discovered new territory and having built some houses on it, is ready to make sure it works correctly before showing it to others.

As you begin this process, have your first draft and any notes or charts you've compiled handy. During your revision you will have a chance to incorporate stylistic techniques for character and plot development examined in the previous chapter. Get focused and read through what you've accomplished while making changes directly in the story.

One thing that will hopefully shine through is the distinct style of your piece. This is called the author's "voice." If you feel that the first draft doesn't quite communicate your individuality, now is the time to improve it.

One way to fine-tune your author's voice is by finding a moment in your story where you can expand on an event. By using flashbacks, foreshadowing, and pacing, you can draw the reader further into your story.

The pacing of your narrative is defined by how the action moves from one event to the next. It is the flow of your story. Find a situation in your story and think about how you can draw it out by slowing it down. This will bring your attention to the minutiae (the small details) of the moment. This slowing of the action will also heighten the story's tension, thereby adding detail to the act. Can you remember a time when you tripped or slipped on something and how it felt as if time were going in slow motion? This is the feeling you want to convey when describing your narrative event.

# Transitions

Transitions are used at the beginning of sentences and paragraphs to promote an engaging flow of events in your story. They keep the reader connected to the action from moment to moment. You might get sick of a favorite song if you've heard it over and over again. It's the same concept in writing. Experiment with starting sentences and paragraphs with different details. You can start with a phrase that describes where you are or how you arrived. Write transitions with the senses in mind, or a description of the surroundings. Example:

**No Rhythm:**
Then he threw me the heavy ball. After that I went to the line.
Then when I heard my name called, I threw the ball at the hoop.
I missed. After that, I sat down.

**Rhythm:**
The ball felt extra heavy when he threw it to me.
I went slowly to the line and waited until I heard my name called.
When I did, I threw the ball at the hoop and missed.
Then I sat back down on the bench.

# Sentence Structure

The way sentences are formed also adds to the tone and flow of writing. A sentence is the vehicle that moves the story along with a sleek motion. By merging sentences in engaging ways, an author achieves a smoother and more interesting story.

A compound sentence is formed when two independent clauses, or single sentences that stand on their own, come together. You can also join like-minded sentences by using punctuation, such as a semicolon. Example:

**The gym felt extremely hot; everyone was still moving around.**

Or a conjunction—words like "and," "or," and "but"—can be used. Example:

**The gym felt extremely hot, but everyone was still moving around.**

# Complex Sentences

An incomplete sentence that makes a statement is known as a dependent clause. It needs to link up with a complete sentence in order to be whole. When you put them together they form a complex sentence.

Dependent clauses can begin with a relative pronoun like "who," "that," or "which." Example:

**The basketball, which felt incredibly heavy, was slippery in my hands.**

The sentence could have stood alone as:

**The basketball was slippery in my hands.**

But adding the dependent clause—"which felt incredibly heavy"—gives it more detail.

A complex sentence can also use a subordinate conjunction to bring together independent and dependent clauses. These are always used at the beginning of a dependent clause and can describe a detail about time (*after*, *before*, *until*), cause and effect (*because*, *since*, *even*, *though*), or a difference between two events (*although*, *while*, *unless*). Example:

## After the basketball tryout was over, people emptied out of the gym.

In this case, *after* sets up cause and effect. Read the following example of a revised draft. In doing so, notice how the author uses a variety of sentence types and lengths. Also, note the rhythm of the writing and its transitional words and phrases.

> As I walked into the gym, I realized how nervous I was about trying out for the basketball team. I hadn't mentioned it to my friends or family because I didn't want them to come to watch. I couldn't forget an earlier time when I blew it. It was during my first summer playing little league. I suddenly heard what sounded like forty of my best friends yelling out my name so loudly that I jumped, missed the pitch, and got hit on my ear, which made me fall down. (It was so embarrassing.)
>
> I heard the squeak of kids' tennis shoes on the gym's floor mixed in with the coach calling out names. When my friend Tommy threw me the ball and it bounced off my knee, it throbbed with pain.

"Lucas Reece," shouted Coach James, "show us what you've got!"

The room went totally quiet and I felt like everyone was staring at me. I was cold and clammy and had a funny taste in my mouth. I bounced the ball a couple of times and hoped it wouldn't slide out of my sweaty hands. The free-throw line looked like it was miles away.

"Be calm," I thought to myself. I took a deep breath, bent my knees, and just as I was about to let the ball loose into the air, my swollen knee buckled as the ball left my hands. I watched it move through the air and felt frozen in place.

Finally, the basketball hit the backboard and just barely went into the hoop. That didn't mean I was on the team, but I hoped that I'd at least be considered.

This example of a revised draft makes use of many stylistic elements. Note its use of the five senses, hyperbole, personification, flashback, foreshadowing, slow motion, and dialogue (both inner and outer) using quotation marks. Notice that when dialogue is used, a new paragraph is started for each character's quotation. Now examine your revised draft for the same elements.

# Proofreading and Editing

Your narrative piece is now in its final stages. Not only have you bolstered the action by using various writing techniques, you've brought out the best in the story by using your distinctive author's voice. Now you will have the chance to proofread and edit your piece by making spelling and punctuation corrections, getting opinions from your peers, and incorporating final changes into your work.

Start with spelling. If you have typed your narrative piece into a computer, engage the spell-checker option and correct any mistakes. If you've written your narrative in longhand, pull out a dictionary to look up any words that you're not sure about. If you have any doubts about a word, look it up. It is also necessary to make the tenses in your verbs match throughout the piece. Check that tense is correct throughout. If your narrative event is happening now, then verbs are in the

## KEY

✔ **Complete a spelling and punctuation check.**

✔ **Add a final title.**

✔ **Polish the story through group effort and constructive feedback.**

✔ **Put the story into its final form.**

present tense. For something that has already happened, go with the past tense, and if you're anticipating a situation, then the future tense is what you need. Example:

**Present Tense: Ellen is excited about her first day of school.**

**Past Tense: Ellen was excited about her first day of school.**

**Future Tense: Ellen will be excited about her first day of school.**

Every element needs to work together smoothly so that your story delivers a clear vision. Make sure that your sentences are complete, meaning that they have a subject (focus/noun) and a predicate (normally a verb that completes the action and/or says something about the subject) and that verbs in all sentences have tenses that match Example of subject and predicate:

**The school principal (subject) was tall (predicate).**

A very simple predicate is a verb.

**The school principal (subject) smiled (predicate).**

Example of subject-verb agreement:

**The classroom is crowded. (Singular verb because it's one room.)**

The people in the classroom are talking loudly.
(Plural verb because there are lots of people.)

# Finishing Touches

Giving your story an appropriate title is important in order to grab the reader's attention. Think about other titles that make you curious. Why do you take notice of them? Does the title offer action? Does it speak about something you relate to? Consider these elements when revising a title for your own writing. Look over your narrative and think about its messages. The tone of your writing will give you an idea of what would best represent your piece, whether your story is suspenseful, dramatic, or anything in between.

You don't want to give everything away, but you do want to deliver a promise about what the reader will find inside the story so that he or she will read on. Example:

*My First Day of School* (working title)

*The Long, Empty Hallways* (drama)

*Losing My Way* (comedic)

It's helpful to read your piece to another person at this stage. Often writers become so involved in their work that it becomes difficult to step outside and see what might be missing or overdone. Meeting with your peers can give you an outsider's perspective. To ensure that your narrative has an interesting mix of elements, find a partner and then trade your writing with him

## Proofreading Symbols

Proofreading marks are used to make corrections to a piece of writing. Here is a guide explaining what the symbols mean.

| | | |
|---|---|---|
| insert a comma | delete | a space needed here |
| apostrophe or single quotation mark | transpose elements | begin new paragraph |
| insert something | close up this space | no paragraph |
| use double quotation marks | use a period here | |

or her. Take four colored markers, each representing a narrative component: red for action; green for dialogue; black for physical descriptions of characters and setting; and blue for inner thoughts, observations, and feelings. Read your partner's work and use the markers to underline items in each sentence.

Once you're finished, return each other's narrative. If you see a rainbow of colors, then you'll know your piece is bal-

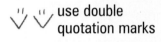

ASK YOURSELF

☐ Have I incorporated all the changes to make my piece better?

☐ Am I ready to present my piece to others?

☐ Have I included a final title that catches readers' interest?

anced, but if you notice that one or more colors are barely used, review your story. Reread it to see how you can add more of those ingredients. Ask questions about your own piece and that of your partner. Think of at least one thing to say that compliments your partner's story.

## A Tense Moment in Class

I was exhausted because I had stayed up all night working on my report. In five minutes I'd have to get up in front of the class to present it and I felt really nervous. My hands were a little sweaty as I put the five pages of my essay about dingoes in the Australian outback in order.

I just hoped that I wouldn't blow it by tripping on my way to the front.

"Ethan Morris," called Ms. Brathwaite.

I cleared my throat and got out of my seat for the long walk to the blackboard. As I went by Alicia Sing, I noticed that she was wearing her cheerleading outfit with her long, dark hair tied up in a ponytail. She looked like she was ready for practice and I got distracted thinking about the football game I was playing on Saturday. But I snapped out of it once I turned around and noticed that everyone in class was staring at me.

> "I hate this," I thought to myself. The classroom looked huge. I took a deep breath and announced my title, "The Unusual Ways of the Dingo." Nobody made a sound, so I kept on reading, trying not to rush it. Finally I was done, and after looking up at my classmates, I made my way back to my seat filled with relief.

# Helping Out

It can be very intimidating to share your writing with classmates, peers, friends, or adults. That's why it's so important to understand how others often feel in the same position. With this in mind, here are some tips for how to use "constructive criticism" in order to help other writers.

Whether the author is reading in front of the class or sharing his or her piece with you directly, pay close attention to what he or she says. Do not yawn or fidget. Look at him or her while he or she is speaking, or if you are reading the piece to yourself, read it carefully.

Write down questions you may have about anything that is confusing to you. Be very mindful of how you phrase your question. Instead of: "Your first sentence didn't make any sense," rephrase it to be more helpful, "I was confused by the first sentence because I didn't understand where the action was taking place."

Just as the phrase implies, your purpose is to be "constructive" by offering helpful ideas to other writers, just as you'd like them to do for you.

# 6 Presentation

Writing is a very independent and imaginative activity. Through perseverance, revision, and a clear vision of what you want to achieve, you've brought your piece to a final stage. This is a moment worthy of congratulations! In the process, aside from family, classmates, and teachers who have possibly seen your narrative in one stage or another, you've had it to yourself. Now you can think about sharing your work with a wider audience.

But before finding places to present your story, you want to make sure your narrative is engaging. Ultimately, the writing is the main thing, but a nice presentation shows that you take pride in your work.

If you have typed your narrative on a computer, make sure the type style (font) and type size are clear and easy to read. This way the reader will only be focused on how entertaining your story is, and not on how your story looks.

If you are writing out your piece on paper, use a blue or black pen and clean white paper with

## KEY

✔ **Polish your piece by adding touches like title changes and slight dialogue changes.**

✔ **Find places to present your finished writing.**

proper margins on either side. The point, again, is to shine the spotlight on your story and not on the method you're using to deliver it.

Claim ownership of your piece by making sure that your name is clearly visible, whether at the top or bottom of the page, or directly underneath the title. Graphics, whether photos or illustrations, can enhance your piece's presentation, but if this is a class assignment, be sure to first check with your teacher.

If you want to use a published picture and your story is going to be printed in a publication, you'll need to get permission from the proper sources. Artists use what is known as copyright, which means that people cannot legally reproduce their work without their consent. An adult can assist you in getting that approved if it's needed.

Look over this final checklist and make sure that you've brought your narrative piece to its ultimate end.

- Is your handwriting, or type style, clear and easy to read?
- Is your story presented on clean paper?
- Are your title and author name visible?
- Are your graphics well presented and do they add to, and not distract from, your story?

## ASK YOURSELF

☐ Does my narrative look interesting and pleasing to the eye?

☐ How can I share my piece with others?

☐ What other narrative subjects could I write about?

**Outlets for Young Writers**

*Stone Soup*
A magazine written entirely by kids. You can view it online at www.stonesoup.com

*Market Guide for Young Writers*
A reference book that lists magazines, book publishers, and contests for young writers. It also provides tips on preparing and submitting stories for publication.

# Spreading the Word

Beyond your immediate circle, there exists a whole community of people who might enjoy reading what you've written.

Since narrative tales focus on storytelling, they are fun to read (and listen to) out loud. Think about presenting your work through a live reading with friends.

Let participants know that they will have only a certain amount of time to read their piece. That way people will come prepared and no one will leave with hurt feelings. To organize a reading, all you need is an appropriate space that is quiet and comfortable.

Another way to share creative stories is through an anthology, which is a collection of writing in book form. You can create a collection of narrative stories featuring your own work or invite others to contribute, too. All you really need to create an anthology of writing is a stapler to bind the stories.

You can make an anthology fancier by adding graphics, or by using a computer to put together a more professional looking anthology. You can even hold a book-signing event where the authors read their work and then sign a copy of the "book" for audience members.

These are just a few ideas. If you'd like to investigate other ways to get people to read your work, search for Web sites for young writers or visit those mentioned in the back of this book.

## Tips for Successful Readings

- Gather a small group to read—usually no more than ten readers. This will keep the audience fresh and will guard against fidgeting.

- Find a space that is quiet and has comfortable seating. Readings can be held in people's homes, backyards, and even parks. But for a public space like a library, you need to obtain permission.

- Discuss in advance the stories that will be read. Decide on a time limit for the readings. Each person should have an equal amount of time and should adjust the length of his or her story appropriately. (Between five and ten minutes is usually sufficient.)

- Hand out homemade invitations about the event stating who, what, when, and where.

- If you're serving refreshments, encourage the audience not to eat during the readings, so there won't be any distractions.

- Most of all have fun!

# Glossary

**anthology** A collection of poems, essays, lyrics, and stories.

**author's voice** The distinct style and personality that every writer brings to his or her work.

**chronological** Relating to the order in which something happened.

**complex sentence** A sentence formed by one independent clause and one or more dependent clauses.

**compound sentence** A sentence in which two independent clauses are joined with a coordinate conjunction.

**conjunction** A word used to connect individual words or groups of words.

**content** The substance of a piece; what is contained in a body of writing.

**copyright** The exclusive right to the publication of literary and artistic work.

**dependent clause** A clause that cannot stand on its own and depends on the rest of a sentence to make a complete sentence.

**dialogue** Conversation between characters in a piece of work.

**expository writing** A piece of writing that gives information.

**fiction** Literature that is created in someone's imagination.

**figure of speech** A device, such as personification, metaphor, or simile, used by authors to create a special meaning.

**first draft** The first version of a story, written without concern about mistakes.

**flashback** A memory of a past experience, often described as a character relives an event that had particular importance in his or her life.

**flash forward** To move the story ahead, anticipating how a situation may turn out.

**foreshadow** A warning or clue about something that will happen later in the story.

**grammar** The guidelines and rules writers follow in order to speak and write in an acceptable manner.

**graphics** Photos or illustrations used to accompany a written story.

**hyperbole** Extreme exaggeration or overstatement used for emphasis.

**independent clause** A clause that expresses a complete thought and can stand alone as a sentence.

**inner dialogue** A character's thoughts that are presented in a way that reveals the person is talking to him or herself.

**margin** The edge, border, or plain space around a page.

**paragraph** A passage of writing, marked by the indentation of the first sentence, that contains a series of related thoughts.

**paraphrase** The rewording of a spoken passage, while retaining its overall meaning.

**personification** A figure of speech in which something that isn't human is given human characteristics.

**phrase** A group of related words that does not express a complete thought.

**plot** The plan of action in a story.

**point of view** The focus of the story from a character's perspective.

**proofreading** Reviewing the final version of a story for any errors.

**quotation marks** Punctuation used to surround direct speech in a story.

**revise** To go back and make changes as needed.

**sensory details** Use of the five senses to describe something.

**slang** Informal speech.

**story map** A graphic organizer used to plan out a piece of writing.

**topic sentence** A sentence describing what the piece of writing will be about.

**transition** Wording or phrasing that smoothly ties two ideas together.

**verb** A word that shows action or links the subject to another word in the sentence.

**working title** The title used for the first draft of a story.

# For More Information

Reading, Writing, and Art Awards
Weekly Reader Corporation
200 First Stamford Place
P.O. Box 120023
Stamford, CT 06912-0023
Web site: http://
www.weeklyreader.com

The Scholastic Art and Writing Awards
555 Broadway
New York, NY 10012
Web site: http://www.scholastic.com

## Web Sites

Due to the changing nature of
Internet links, the Rosen Publishing
Group, Inc., has developed an
online list of Web sites related to
the subject of this book. This site is
updated regularly. Please use this
link to access the list:

http://www.rosenlinks.com/lws/nawr

# Getting Published

*Merlyn's Pen*
Fiction, Essays, and Poems by
    America's Teens
P.O. Box 910
East Greenwich, RI 02818-0964
Web site: http://www.merlynspen.com

*Skipping Stones*
Multicultural Children's Magazine
P.O. Box 3939
Eugene, OR 97403-0939
Web site: http://
www.skippingstones.org

*Stone Soup*
A Magazine by Young Writers
    and Artists
P.O. Box 83
Santa Cruz, CA 95063
Web site: http://www.stonesoup.com

*TeenInk*
P.O. Box 30
Newton, MA 02161 Web site:
http://www.teenink.com

*Teen Voices*
P.O. Box 120-027
Boston, MA 02112-0027
Web site: http://www.teenvoices.com

*Young Voices Magazine*
P.O. Box 2321
Olympia, WA 98507
Web site: http://www.youngvoices
  magazine.com

# For Further Reading

Calham, Ruth. *6 + 1 Traits of Writing: The Complete Guide*. New York: Scholastic, 2003.

Kemper, Dave; Patrick Sebranek; and Verne Meyer. *All Write: A Student Handbook for Writing and Learning*. Wilmington, MA: Great Source Education Group, 2002.

Mandelbaum, Paul, ed. *First Words: Earliest Writing from Favorite Contemporary Authors*. Chapel Hill, NC: Algonquin Books, 2000.

Sunley, Laura. *Fun with Grammar: 75 Quick Activities & Games That Help Kids Learn About Nouns, Verbs, Adjectives, Adverbs, and More*. New York: Scholastic, 2002

# Bibliography

Ace Writing. "The Writing Process." 2002. Retrieved July 7, 2003 (http://www.geocities.com/fifth_grade_tpes/index.html)

English Biz. "Writing to Describe and Original Writing." 2003. Retrieved October 16, 2003 (http://www.englishbiz.co.uk/mainguides/describe.htm).

Feder, Barnaby J., "With the Apples Arriving by E-Mail, Teachers Adapt." *New York Times*, August 14, 2003, p. G5.

Guernsey, Lisa. "A Young Writer's Roundtable, via the Web." *New York Times*, August 14, 2003, p. G1.

"Guide to Grammar and Writing." 2003. Retrieved August 1, 2003 (http://webster.commnet.edu/grammar/index.htm).

Hewitt, John. "Fifteen Craft Exercises for Writers." Writers Resource Center Online. Retrieved June 25, 2003 (http://www.poewar.com/articles/15_exercises.htm).

Kemper, Dave; Patrick Sebranek; and Verne Meyer. *All Write: A Student Handbook for Writing and Learning*. Wilmington, MA: Great Source Education Group, 1998.

LEO: Literacy Education Online. "The Write Place Catalogue." 1997. Retrieved July 10, 2003 (http://leo.stcloudstate.edu/acadwrite/descriptive.html).

Scholastic for Teachers. "Writing with Writers." 2003. Retrieved June 20, 2003 (http://teacher.scholastic.com/writewit/).

*Stone Soup*. "Links for Young Writers." 2004. Retrieved June 20, 2003 (http://www.stonesoup.com/main2/links.html).

Teacher Created Materials. "Language Arts." 2000. Retrieved July 21, 2003 (http://www.teachercreated.com).

Winthrop, Elizabeth. "Some Practical Advice on Writing and Publishing for Young Writers." 1998. Retrieved August 26, 2003 (http://www.elizabethwinthrop.com/advice.html)

# Index

## About the Author

Lauren Spencer is originally from California and now lives in New York City, where she teaches writing workshops in the public schools. She also writes lifestyle and music articles for magazines.

## Credits

**Designer:** Geri Fletcher; **Editor:** Joann Jovinelly